The
Bible Lesson
Pocket Book

Quick bible lessons for the busy minister and teacher...

Rev. Dr. E. J. Fleming, Jr.

Written by:
Rev. Dr. E. J. Fleming, Jr.

Printed by:
CreateSpace
4900 LaCross Road
North Charleston, SC 29406
www.createspace.com

**The Bible Lesson Pocket Book: Quick bible lessons
for the busy minister and teacher, Second edition,**
published by Foundations for Hope
11601 Shadow Creek Pkwy
Ste. 111-275
Pearland, TX 77584

Unless otherwise noted, biblical words were
researched and described using
Strong's Hebrew and Greek Lexicon.

ISBN-13: 978-0692494509
ISBN-10: 0692494502

DEDICATION

This book is dedicated to all sincere, serious, and studious ministers and teachers of God's Word who find themselves constantly challenged with not having enough time to spend in prayer and study due to balancing a multiplicity of responsibilities.

ABOUT THIS BOOK

This book is a compilation of short bible lessons which can be taught in twenty minutes or less. An agenda is listed at the beginning of each lesson to provide structure for the teaching session.

In addition, not only is this book is a great resource for busy ministers and teachers, it is also a great resource for first time bible teachers and individuals who are just entering into the ministry. The lessons contained herein are essentially core "bare bones" material that can be either taught "As-Is" or expounded upon as prayerfully led by the Holy Spirit.

TABLE OF CONTENTS

ACKNOWLEDGMENTS

First, I want to thank God who has given me the time and vision to write this book. Second, I want to thank my parents, Mr. and Mrs. Eddie Fleming, Sr. who instilled in me and my siblings the value of education and hard work. As I worked to complete this book, I am reminded of something my mother told me when I first started preaching over twenty years ago from the time of this writing, "When people come to church all they want to know is what the bible says…" Third, I want to thank my wife, children, siblings, and host of family, friends, pastors, and colleagues who have encouraged and supported me throughout the years. My wife and children have been my extra right hand and I thank God for them. Finally, I would be remiss not to mention my late grandmother whom the family affectionately called "Na-Na". The Lord used her as she was instrumental in me receiving a lot of preaching engagements when I first started preaching. Those were valuable moments of learning and growth.

STRUGGLING WITH A WEAK FAITH

Agenda:
- Greeting and Prayer
- Scripture
- Lesson
- Discussion
- Prayer Request
- Closing Prayer

Greeting and Prayer
Start session by welcoming attendees and saying an opening prayer. You may also ask one of the attendees if they would like to say the opening prayer.

Scripture ~ Mark 4:35-41
And the same day, when the even was come, he saith unto them, Let us pass over unto the other side. And when they had sent away the multitude, they took him even as he was in the ship. And there were also with him other little ships. And there arose a great storm of wind, and the waves beat into the ship, so that it was now full. And he was in the hinder part of the ship, asleep on a pillow: and they

awake him, and say unto him, Master, carest thou not that we perish? And he arose, and rebuked the wind, and said unto the sea, Peace, be still. And the wind ceased, and there was a great calm. And he said unto them, Why are ye so fearful? how is it that ye have no faith? And they feared exceedingly, and said one to another, What manner of man is this, that even the wind and the sea obey him? [1]

Into the lesson…

Some of you may already be familiar with this passage of scripture. The disciples had just dismissed a crowd who stood along the shores of the Galilean sea as Jesus taught them from a ship. Upon dismissal, Jesus said to the disciples, let us pass over to the other side. As they sailed, a great storm of wind arose and waves beat into the ship so that it was now full (of water)… While all this is happening, Jesus is asleep on a pillow in the back of the ship. With this in mind, have you ever encountered a situation, or one of life's storms and felt as if you were going through it by yourself? If you be honest with yourself, have you ever been going through and wondered if Jesus has abandoned you or fell asleep on your situation?

These disciples, some of them experienced fishermen, probably did everything they could possibly think of to get the water out of their ship – maybe they even tossed some cargo overboard. However, as time went on, although Jesus was with them, somehow, the thought of death set in - and they woke Him up… They didn't say, "Jesus, the ship is filled with water." They didn't say, "Jesus, we need your help, we are sinking." They ask Him a question – and in that same question accused Him. "Master, carest thou

---

[1] *The Holy Bible: King James Version.* (2009). (Electronic Edition of the 1900 Authorized Version., Mk 4:35–41). Bellingham, WA: Logos Research Systems, Inc.

not that we perish?"

Upon hearing their cry of distress and accusation, Jesus "arose, and rebuked the wind, and said unto the sea, *Peace, be still.* And the wind ceased, and there was a great calm. And he said unto them, *Why are ye so fearful? how is it that ye have no faith?*"

Just as it was with these disciples so it is with many of us. There are times in our lives when we encounter circumstances that are beyond our control and the true condition or strength of our faith is revealed. The wind storm blowing and ship being filled with water uncovered two things regarding the faith of the disciples. First, they were fearful. Second, they had not a weak faith – but faith was totally absent for Jesus asked, "How is it that you have NO faith?"

For many of us, we demonstrate faith in some areas of our lives, then in other areas our faith is either weak or totally absent. As quiet as it is kept, many Christians struggle with having a case of weak faith thus allowing their situations to get the best of them. A good indicator as to whether or not you may possess a case of weak faith (or no faith) is if you take matters into your own hands instead of trusting God.

Many times, we deceive ourselves by saying our faith is stronger than we are willing to admit. Yet, deep down inside, we know we have some struggles. So, often times, storms and trials have a way of pulling back the covers – and help us to see ourselves and where we stand in our relationship with Jesus Christ. Do we trust Him or do we not trust Him at all? Having faith or total dependence and trust in Jesus is a matter of surrender and casting all of our cares upon Him. Even if Jesus takes a nap, He's still in control and the Master of our seas of circumstances.

Conclusion:

Just as Jesus spoke to winds and seas, He can speak to all of your situations and give you peace... All you have to do is trust Him.

Questions for discussion...

- Have you ever encountered a situation whereby you thought or felt as if Jesus was sleep or simply didn't care? If so, do you mind sharing? (*As an icebreaker, you may want to start by sharing your own experience.*)

- Reflecting on the previous questions, how did you respond?

- What are some ways in which we can respond in faith to our storms in life?

Prayer request...
Ask students if they have any prayer request...

Closing prayer...
Below is a sample prayer that can be used or you can use your own incorporating the prayer request of the bible study attendees...

Dear God our Father, we admit that there are times we struggle regarding our faith. Help us today to trust you as we should – that You have not abandoned us. Thank You for Your omnipotent grace and love. As the wind of trials beat against us, let us remember to call on You and not lean unto our own understanding. Help us in all of our ways to acknowledge You - that You may direct our paths. In Jesus name we pray, Amen.

LESSON 2
TAKING MATTERS INTO YOUR OWN HANDS

Agenda:
- Greeting and Opening Prayer
- Scripture
- Lesson
- Discussion
- Prayer Request
- Closing Prayer

Greeting and Prayer
Start session by welcoming attendees and saying an opening prayer. You may also ask one of the attendees if they would like to say the opening prayer.

Scripture ~ Philippians 4:6-7
Be careful for nothing; but in every thing by prayer and supplication with thanksgiving let your requests be made known unto God. And the peace of God, which passeth all understanding, shall keep your

hearts and minds through Christ Jesus.[1]

Into the lesson…

Considering the Apostle's Paul's situation, this statement he writes to the church in Philippi carries a lot of weight. Throughout his ministry, he has endured hardship. He had been beaten, and even left for dead. Yet, his desire was to go to Rome and declare the unsearchable riches of God or preach the Gospel. His journey to Rome was not a pleasant one. He was taken there in chains as a prisoner. The vessel that he was on was shipwrecked. He wrote this letter to the Philippian church while under house arrest in Rome to express his appreciation for the kindness towards him during his sentence.[2] Although Paul has endured so much and is under house arrest, in verse 4 of the same chapter he admonishes Christians to rejoice in the Lord always…

When circumstances are not to our liking, rejoicing can be difficult. Paul has been beaten, left for dead, mistreated, taken prisoner and now under house arrest. Yet, he is telling others to rejoice in the *Lord* always…. Then he adds by stating…

> *Be careful (be anxious – or troubled) for nothing (or no thing); but in every thing by prayer (conversation with God) and supplication (asking humbly) with thanksgiving let your requests be made known unto God. And the peace of God, which passeth all understanding,*

---

[1] *The Holy Bible: King James Version.* (2009). (Electronic Edition of the 1900 Authorized Version., Php 4:6–7). Bellingham, WA: Logos Research Systems, Inc.

[2] Scriptures regarding Paul's plight can be found in the Book of Acts as well as in 2 Cor. chapters 4 and 11.

shall keep your hearts and minds through Christ Jesus.[3]

In this passage, when situations arise, what we are being instructed to do is not take matters in our own hands. Often times, the worst place for a situation to be is in our hands. Be troubled by *no* thing, but in everything by prayer and supplication – with thanksgiving let your request be made known to God. Whatever your situation is, give it to God – place it in His hands and in return we will receive a peace from God that surpasses all understanding. However, if you take matters into your own hands, in most cases, you very well may forfeit the peace that only God can give.

Conclusion:

When we take matters into our own hands, instead of turning to God first, often times it complicates things and makes the situation worse. The best thing to do in all things is to go to God first.

Questions for discussion…

- What are some things people have a tendency to hold on to that they need to give to God?

- Often times when we are wronged or mistreated, there is a tendency to want to get even. Sometimes people want the one who has wronged them to feel their pain. What are some things the bible say about this? As a help to this questions, the following verse is one of many the bible gives

---

[3] *The Holy Bible: King James Version.* Php 4:6–7.

regarding taking matters into your own hands.

> *Repay no one evil for evil, but give thought to do what is honorable in the sight of all. If possible, so far as it depends on you, live peaceably with all. Beloved, never avenge yourselves, but leave it to the wrath of God, for it is written, "Vengeance is mine, I will repay, says the Lord." To the contrary, "if your enemy is hungry, feed him; if he is thirsty, give him something to drink; for by so doing you will heap burning coals on his head." Do not be overcome by evil, but overcome evil with good.* [4] (Ro 12:17-21)

- What are some things you can do to ensure that you have allowed the Lord to handle your situation?

Prayer request...
Ask students if they have any prayer request...

Closing prayer...
Below is a sample prayer that can be used or you can use your own incorporating the prayer request of the bible study attendees...

Dear God our Father, we admit that there are times we want to take matters into our own hands. Help us to take our burdens to You in prayer and leave them in Your mighty hands. And in exchange, You promise to give us a peace that surpasses all understanding. Help us to pray for our enemies – those who despitefully use and abuse Your children. Help us to remember that we are all Your

---

[4] *The Holy Bible: English Standard Version.* (2001). (Ro 12:17–21). Wheaton: Standard Bible Society.

children and our actions should always reflect that – for we stand as examples, even in the face of our enemies. Thank You for Your omnipotent grace and love. Help us in all of our ways to acknowledge You - that You may direct our paths.

In Jesus name we pray, Amen.

LESSON 3
STEPS FOR FINDING JOY

Agenda:
- Greeting and Opening Prayer
- Scripture
- Lesson
- Discussion
- Prayer Request
- Closing Prayer

Greeting and Prayer
Start session by welcoming attendees and saying an opening prayer. You may also ask one of the attendees if they would like to say the opening prayer.

Scripture ~ John 15:1-11
I am the true vine, and my Father is the husbandman. Every branch in me that beareth not fruit he taketh away: and every branch that beareth fruit, he purgeth it, that it may bring forth more fruit. Now ye are clean through the word which I have spoken unto you. Abide in me, and I in you. As the branch cannot bear fruit of itself, except it abide in the vine; no more can ye, except ye abide in me. I am the

vine, ye are the branches: He that abideth in me, and I in him, the same bringeth forth much fruit: for without me ye can do nothing. If a man abide not in me, he is cast forth as a branch, and is withered; and men gather them, and cast them into the fire, and they are burned. If ye abide in me, and my words abide in you, ye shall ask what ye will, and it shall be done unto you. Herein is my Father glorified, that ye bear much fruit; so shall ye be my disciples. As the Father hath loved me, so have I loved you: continue ye in my love. If ye keep my commandments, ye shall abide in my love; even as I have kept my Father's commandments, and abide in his love.

These things have I spoken unto you, that my joy might remain in you, and that your joy might be full.[1]

Into the lesson…

In this pericope of scripture, we find Jesus sharing with His disciples the importance of staying connected to Him. In doing so, He uses as an analogy: a vine, a branch, and fruit. The vine represents Jesus, we are the branches, and the fruit is a product that results from the branch being connected to the vine.

The moral or impetus of the passage is that unless the branch is connected to the vine, it cannot produce any fruit. So, the question we must ask ourselves is, "Am I connected to the Vine?" If we are connected and we are bearing fruit, the bible says that God (the Father), who is also the Husbandman or the owner of the vineyard. He purgeth it – verse 2. Why? He does this that the branch may bring forth, not a piece of fruit or some fruit, but *much* fruit.

Now, the purging process is not an exciting one

---

[1] *The Holy Bible: King James Version.* (2009). (Electronic Edition of the 1900 Authorized Version., Jn 15). Bellingham, WA: Logos Research Systems, Inc.

because it means that some cutting has to be done. Every now and then, for God to get the best or more out of us, He may have to cut some people or things out of our lives. He may have to rearrange our schedules or change our plans. Sometimes He allows us to experience heartaches and setbacks… We encounter people who mean things for evil – but God meant it for our good. No matter what you encounter in life, always remember it is always in the best interest of God who is our owner, to get the best out of that in which He owns – which is us… So, if you are a child of God, just remember, weeping may be endured for a night but joy cometh in the morning.[2]

Although quite often purging is painful, the outset at times is disappointing, and we may not understand what is going on, all God is trying to do is set you up for a blessing. Let's look at verses seven and eight: "7If ye abide (stay) in me (stay in fellowship – stay connected – don't throw in the towel), and *my words abide in you*, ye shall ask what ye will, and it shall be done unto you. 8 Herein is my Father glorified, that ye bear much fruit; so shall ye be my disciples."

The Jesus goes on to say, "As the Father hath loved (to be fond of – cherish with unreasoning feelings) me, so have I loved you: continue ye in my love. 10 If ye keep my commandments, ye shall abide (stay) in my love (kindness, benevolence – goodwill); even as I have kept my Father's commandments, and abide (stay) in his love (kindness, benevolence – goodwill)."

Steps for finding joy…

Step 1 – Have a relationship with Jesus Christ.
In verse eleven, Jesus states, "These things have I

---

[2] *The Holy Bible: King James Version.* Ps. 30:5

spoken unto you, that my joy might remain in you, and *that* your joy might be full". So, if you feel as if you are running low on joy, check your connection with Jesus. Having a sound relationship with Jesus Christ is the prerequisite for experiencing joy.

Step 2 – Know that Jesus desires for you to be filled with joy. [11] These things *have I spoken unto you, that my joy might remain in you*, and *that* your joy might be *full*.

Step 3 – Understand that happiness is based on happenings. Joy is based on your connection to the True Vine – which is Jesus Christ. Happiness and happenings are based on externalities or what is going on around us. Joy is based on internalities, what we have on the inside. When we are connected to the True Vine – Jesus Christ, we have a joy that is not moved or swayed by object circumstances (or happenings).

Illustration…

Some time ago, I got into my truck and it wouldn't start. It was filled with gas. I haven't had any problems with it. The lights came on and horn blew - but it still wouldn't start. So, I opened the hood and to my surprise, I had some corrosion around the battery terminal – I had a bad connection. I had a truck but couldn't go anywhere. Lights and horn worked but the truck wouldn't start. It wasn't until I got rid of the corrosion around the terminal and got a good connection that the truck started. That may be somebody today. You've been going and going – but you've come to a place where things are not starting like they should. You have some build up around your terminals that's keeping you from getting a good connection with the Power Source.

Conclusion:

There may be some things that have built up and it's interfering with your connection to the Lord. In light of what may be causing that interference (job, goals, friends, habits, pain from the past), He desires that you and He be connected. Like myself when my truck wouldn't start, you may find yourself just going and going then stranded – all appears well but when was the last time you checked under the hood? How's that connection with the Power Source, Jesus Christ looking? Any corrosion? Let Jesus clean away any corrosion that may have built up and is interfering with your connection to Him – let Him cut away those things that may be keeping you from living to your fullest potential. He wants the best for your life – He wants you to be filled with His joy…

Questions for discussion…

- Where does joy come from?

- Is there a difference between joy and happiness? If so, then what is it?

- Can you have joy without being connected to Jesus Christ?

- Is happiness temporary? If yes, then what are some ways people try to find happiness?

- Jesus states He share these things so that our joy might be full. Why do you think He wants us to be filled with joy?

- Reflecting on the previous question, do you think some people choose to be joyless?

Prayer request...
Ask students if they have any prayer request...

Closing prayer...
Below is a sample prayer that can be used or you can use your own incorporating the prayer request of the bible study attendees...

Dear God our Father, often times we wrestle in our pursuit of happiness, only to find ourselves unhappier, dissatisfied, and depressed. Sometimes we settle for a fleeting moment of fun rather than turning to You. Help us to turn to You that we may be filled with Your joy. Lord, we thank You for Your words of comfort and restoration. Help us to remember that You only want the best for us and have the best in store for us. Thank You for Your omnipotent grace and love. Help us in all of our ways to acknowledge You – that You may direct our paths.

In Jesus name we pray, Amen.

WHERE OR IN WHOM DO YOU PLACE YOUR TRUST?

Agenda:
- Greeting and Opening Prayer
- Scripture
- Lesson
- Discussion
- Prayer Request
- Closing Prayer

Greeting and Prayer
Start session by welcoming attendees and saying an opening prayer. You may also ask one of the attendees if they would like to say the opening prayer.

Scripture ~ Proverbs 3:5-6
Trust in the LORD with all thine heart; and lean not unto thine own understanding. In all thy ways acknowledge him, and he shall direct

thy paths. [1]

Into the lesson…

Solomon, the wisest man who ever lived. When you read about him in the Old Testament and all of his possessions, I would venture to even say that he was also the richest man who ever lived. It is interesting that one who had so much wealth and wisdom would make this statement – lean not unto thine own understanding. Often times, people who have a lot and know a lot tend to be self-reliant – and trusting in God is usually an afterthought or only happens when object circumstances arise. Many find themselves only turning to God when circumstances grow beyond their control. Regarding this, Proverbs 3:6 says "in all thy ways acknowledge Him" and the promise is that the Creator of the universe (the Lord) will direct your paths…

In an article entitled Faith v/s Trust[2] the following is stated…

> *Quite often the words faith and trust are tossed about in religious circles. These words are used like salt, seasoning any dialogue with a distinctly "Christian" flavor. But what do they mean? Is faith the same thing as trust? If not, what is the difference?*

---

[1] *The Holy Bible: King James Version.* (2009). (Electronic Edition of the 1900 Authorized Version., Pr 3:4–6). Bellingham, WA: Logos Research Systems, Inc.

[2] Ben. *Faith vs. Trust.* http://christianity.yoexpert.com/christianity-general/what-is-the-difference-between-faith-and-trust-20479.html (accessed May 13, 2015).

Faith is a noun.

It is something we HAVE... As (the Lord) reveals Himself and His Love to us, this "knowing" of Him in our head (knowledge), and in our heart (beliefs), is the substance, our evidence, of Him and His Love (Hebrews 11:1 "Now faith is the substance of things hoped for, the evidence of things not seen.").

Faith says "I know Him, and I believe!"...

but faith is not trust...

Trust is a verb.

Trust is something we DO...

Trust is faith in action! It is the manifestation of our faith in our thoughts and actions. While faith says "He can...", trust says "He is... and I will think and act accordingly!"

It is far easier to have faith in God; there are unbelievers who have this. It is a lot harder to exercise trust in Him...

A short analogy (...though based on a real story):

The Great Blondin

In the late 1800's there was a great performer named Jean Francois Gravelot. He was known as "The Great Blondin." He was a "daredevil" of sorts; a tightrope walker specifically.

One of his greatest stunts, involved walking a tightrope high above the world famous Niagara Falls. Blondin performed this death-defying feat more than once, adding elements of difficulty each time. Once he even carried his manager on his back!

Blondin was quite the showman, he had a knack for engaging the crowd, stirring the suspense and excitement. Upon completing one attempt, he asked the crowd if they believed a second attempt would be a successful one. The crowd unanimously agreed it would. Always looking to better his last great feat, Blondin now asked the crowd if they believed he could cross the falls on the tightrope while pushing a wheelbarrow. Having seen his previous stunt, and how seemingly easy it was for him, the crowd had no doubt he could pull off this new, more difficult one. Again, the response was unanimous, the crowd had no doubt "The Great Blondin" could do it!

Blondin was ready to attempt this amazing feat that only he could do, but before he set out on the rope, he had one last question for the crowd: "Which of you will ride in the wheelbarrow?" The crowd was frozen, still, silent. Not a single man or woman responded to his challenge...

All of those people witnessed Blondin cross the falls on the rope. They gained first-hand knowledge of his abilities. They had a well-founded belief that he could perform the more difficult stunt. Yet, when it came time to act on those beliefs, they were silent...still. They did not trust him.

Many of us have seen what God can do, and we believe (faith)... when He calls us to "ride" with him (trust), will we sit silent? Will we stand still?

Conclusion:

The following questions are being posed for you to think about *where and in whom* do you place your trust. You may have professed that you have faith in the Lord but where or in whom do you place your trust? Are you placing it in people, things, your own abilities, the right set of circumstances? You believe in what God can do and His incomparable power but do you trust Him to work out your circumstances. Do you trust Him enough to ride in His wheelbarrow?

> *Trust (confide or have confidence) in the LORD with all*
> *thine heart; and lean not unto thine own*
> *understanding.*
> *In all thy ways acknowledge him,*
> *And he shall direct thy paths. [3]*

Questions for discussion...

- What is the difference between faith and trust?

- Do you think people struggle with trusting God? If so, why?

- Do you think people struggle with having faith in God? If so, why?

- What is the danger placing one's trust and/or faith into things, people, or self?

- What does it mean to acknowledge God in all our ways?

- How can we acknowledge God in all our ways?

Prayer request...
Ask attendees if they have any prayer request...

---

[3] *The Holy Bible: King James Version.* Pr 3:4–6.

Closing prayer...
Below is a sample prayer that can be used or you can use your own incorporating the prayer request of the bible study attendees...

Dear God our Father, often we lean unto our own understanding and address matters according to our own volition. Many times we say that we believe in You but far too often fail to totally trust You. Help us to move from trusting You in some areas and not in others to trusting You in all things. Let us not forget that the first step to doing this is acknowledging You in all things and the promise is that You will direct our paths. Thank You for being patient and merciful towards us in that You have not given up on us when we failed to trust in You. Now, may the words of our mouth and the meditations of our heart be holy and acceptable in Thy sight.

In Jesus name we pray, Amen.

LESSON 5
HAVING A MADE UP MIND

Agenda:
- Greeting and Opening Prayer
- Scripture
- Lesson
- Discussion
- Prayer Request
- Closing Prayer

Greeting and Prayer
Start session by welcoming attendees and saying an opening prayer. You may also ask one of the attendees if they would like to say the opening prayer.

Scripture ~ James1:8
A double minded man is unstable in all his ways. [1]

---

[1] *The Holy Bible: King James Version.* (2009). (Electronic Edition of the 1900 Authorized Version., Jas 1:8). Bellingham, WA: Logos Research Systems, Inc.

Into the lesson...

The book of James was written by "James" who was the brother of Jesus. Scholars say that he became a leader of the church in Jerusalem, and presided at the Jerusalem council.   In his writing, he addresses the issue of double mindedness or double-souled. In studying this, this term "double mindedness" means more than just having your thoughts on two different things and can't choose between either. It means to be fickle and wavering in one's relationship with God – it means to have divided loyalties. It takes hypocrisy (or falsehood) to another level. In other words, a double – minded person has their heart towards God and their heart towards other things both at the same time – as a result, all of their heart is not towards God. Even though they would claim that their heart is bent towards God, at the same times, this individual is holding on to some activities and thoughts that are not in line with God's word. The Greek word for double-minded is "dipsychos" which means two psyches – or, two-minds. This denotes dual spiritual personalities. When encountering a person as such, you never know which one you are dealing with. The bible says this person, this man, woman, boy, or girl is unstable – or inconsistent in not just a few things but in all their ways. Revelations 3:15-17 describe this individual as a "luke-warm" believer. It reads:

> *I know thy works, that thou art neither cold nor hot: I would thou wert cold or hot. So then because thou art lukewarm, and neither cold nor hot, I will spue thee out of my mouth. Because thou sayest, I am rich, and increased with goods, and have need of nothing; and knowest not that thou art wretched, and miserable, and poor, and blind, and naked* [2]

[2] *The Holy Bible: King James Version.* Re 3:15–17.

In summation of this passage, a letter has been sent to the church and Jesus is saying I wish you were hot or cold – but you're neither – you are in the middle; therefore, I will spit or spew you out of my mouth. According to the scripture, this type of person is deceived because they assume that things are alright due to what they have and how things are going for them. However, they don't know that they are wretched, miserable, and poor, and blind, and naked.

We find the remedy for double-mindedness in James 4:7-8.

> *Submit (Give) yourselves therefore to God. Resist the devil, and he will flee from you. Draw nigh to God, and he will draw nigh to you. Cleanse your hands, ye sinners; and purify your hearts, ye double minded.*[3]

Conclusion:

The Lord gives us a choice regarding how we live our lives. We can choose to live for Him or not. There is no in-between or middle ground. The decision to even claim neutrality in this matter is a decision in and of itself to not live for the Master.

> *And if it seem evil unto you to serve the LORD, choose you this day whom ye will serve; whether the gods which your fathers served that were on the other side of the flood, or the gods of the Amorites, in whose land ye dwell: but as for me and my house, we will serve the LORD.* [4]

---

[3] *The Holy Bible: King James Version.* Jas 4:6–8.

[4] Ibid., Jos 24:15.

Questions for discussion...

- Give some reasons why people are double-minded in their walk with God?

- Provide some examples of double-mindedness.

- What are the pitfalls of being double-minded?

- Is double-mindedness curable? If so, what is the remedy?

Prayer request...
Ask attendees if they have any prayer request...

Closing prayer...
Below is a sample prayer that can be used or you can use your own incorporating the prayer request of the bible study attendees...

Dear God our Father, often we struggle in trusting You. Help us to have a made up mind. Every now and then we all waver and show signs of double-mindedness. Help us to acknowledge You in all that we set out to accomplish trusting You to even catch us if it is Your will that we just leap into the dark. Every now and then we waiver in our thoughts. Draw our wandering minds in on You, Your love, and Your grace. Thank You for the reminders that You have given us in Your word to help us get back on track when we stray – continue to direct us this day as well as in the days to come.

In Jesus name we pray, Amen.

WHERE ARE YOU NOW?

Agenda:
- Greeting and Opening Prayer
- Scripture
- Lesson
- Discussion
- Prayer Request
- Closing Prayer

Greeting and Prayer
Start session by welcoming attendees and saying an opening prayer. You may also ask one of the attendees if they would like to say the opening prayer.

Scripture ~ Hebrews 12:5
For when for the time ye ought to be teachers, ye have need that one teach you again which be the first principles of the oracles of God; and

are become such as have need of milk, and not of strong meat. [1]

Into the lesson...

Where are you now? It is incumbent that we as Christians find time to consider where we are regarding our relationship with Christ. Where do we stand regarding our commitments to the things of the Lord?

Like taking a road trip, we often take time to consider how many miles we have traveled since we left our point of origination in order to gage how much further we need to go in order to reach our destination. Depending on where we are, determines if any adjustments need to be made as we travel. Do we need to get some gas, are the tires in good condition, is the car running hot, are we tired and need to rest, is the weather conducive for travel, is the traffic light or heavy, is there any road construction? All of these things at some point are taken into consideration when we think about where we are when we travel.

Just as we consider where we are or our location as we travel the highways, we also must assess where we are as we travel from earth to glory. Spiritually, where are you right now? Do you need a spiritual fill-up or tune-up? Are you were you need to be or are you running behind? This is what the author of Hebrews is calling attention to in our text. There were those who had been in church for a while, but they had not progressed to where they were expected to be at this point in their spiritual lives. According to the scriptures, they should have been teachers by now but instead they were needing someone to still teach them the fundamentals of the Christian faith.

---

[1] *The Holy Bible: King James Version.* (2009). (Electronic Edition of the 1900 Authorized Version., Heb 5:12). Bellingham, WA: Logos Research Systems, Inc.

This passage calls upon all blood-bought born again believers to think about where they are spiritually. Are you were you should be? How long have you been professing Christ as Savior? God holds us all accountable regarding our spiritual whereabouts? Genesis 3, God asked Adam, "Adam, where art thou?" It was because of sin, Adam wasn't where he was supposed to be. What about you? What about me? 1 Kings 19, Elijah, the man of God, after performing a great miracle, queen Jezebel wanted to kill him. Fearing for his life, he fled to another town leaving his servant behind. What about you? What about me? Jonah 1, God called Jonah to preach to the Ninevites. However, because he'd rather see them receive God's condemnation – and perhaps even due to fear, instead of going to Nineveh, he hid himself at the bottom of a ship that was headed to a different city. What about you? What about me?

All of us have ups and downs, special personal prayer needs, family and friends who need to be lifted up in prayer (And although in 1 Peter 5:6-7 we are instructed to "Humble yourselves therefore under the mighty hand of God, that he may exalt you in due time: Casting all your care upon him; for he careth for you."[2], when was the last time a little spiritual inventory was performed? You can be lost and don't know it… You can be behind and don't know it. Performing inventory of our "spiritual whereabouts" is a matter of stewardship.

Conclusion:

In order to have an idea of where you are, you must know from whence you've started and where you are going. Quite often many start well but along the way lose

---

[2] *The Holy Bible: King James Version.* 1 Pe 5:6–7.

sight of where they are heading. Without consistently monitoring progress in any endeavor, we are bound for stagnation - especially when it comes to our relationship with Jesus Christ and overall spiritual maturity.

Questions for discussion...

- Often times we are asked, "Where do we see ourselves within the next three to five years?" Do you think it would help to ask the same question regarding our spirituality or ministry endeavors?

- What do you think can contribute to stunted or stagnant spiritual maturity?

- Reflecting upon the length of time you have been a Christian, do you feel or believe that you are where you should be in your ministry endeavors? If yes, "why?" If no, "why not?"

- What are some things one can do to help themselves to grow spiritually?

Prayer request...
Ask attendees if they have any prayer request...

Closing prayer...
Below is a sample prayer that can be used or you can use your own incorporating the prayer request of the bible study attendees...

Dear God our Father, often we are constantly on-the-go and very seldom pause to think about where we are spiritually. We even may be on the verge of having a blow out in the road of life and don't know it. Help us to pause and reflect on You, Your Word, and where we are? Help us to stay on the straight and narrow path. We thank You for Your grace and mercy. Help us not to become so busy in doing that we forget about being or fail to be what You want us to become. Thank You for Your omnipotent grace and love – direct us this day as well as in the days to come.

In Jesus name we pray, Amen.

LESSON 7
STANDING IN YOUR OWN WAY

Agenda:
- Greeting and Opening Prayer
- Scripture
- Lesson
- Discussion
- Prayer Request
- Closing Prayer

Greeting and Prayer
Start session by welcoming attendees and saying an opening prayer. You may also ask one of the attendees if they would like to say the opening prayer.

Scripture ~ Proverbs 14:12
There is a way which seemeth right unto a man, But the end thereof are the ways of death. [1]

---

[1] *The Holy Bible: King James Version.* (2009). (Electronic Edition of the 1900 Authorized Version., Pr 14:11–12). Bellingham, WA: Logos Research Systems, Inc.

Into the lesson…

The book of proverbs is a collection of wise and pithy statements. Many of the sayings found therein are attributed to the authorship of King Solomon who has been coined as the wisest (and maybe even the wealthiest) man who ever lived. It can be inferred that the passage in which this lesson is based unfortunately is portrayed in the life of Solomon - for there were some decisions he made that ultimately put a strain on his relationship with God. Like Solomon, many men and women have found their lives going in a downward spiral as a result of the choices they have made – or taking risk they believed were harmless because nothing happening the first or second time.

The first part of this passage states that there is a way which seemeth right unto a man… The word "seemeth" infers that whatever *way* one think is right is actually *not* right. It looks "ok" but it is not "ok". It feels "good" but it is not "good". It looks "well" but it is not "well".

Most, if not all of us, at some point or another have found ourselves going in a direction or making a choice that seemed right. We find a classic example of this in Genesis chapter three. God instructed Adam to not eat of the forbidden fruit. Evidently, he shared with Eve what God said as well as the consequence because she stated the same to the serpent. After which the serpent planted a seed of doubt in her mind by stating:

> *Ye shall not surely die: For God doth know that in the day ye eat thereof, then your eyes shall be opened, and ye shall be as gods, knowing good and evil. And when the woman saw that the tree was good for food, and that it was pleasant to the eyes, and a tree to be desired to make one wise, she took of the fruit thereof, and did eat, and*

gave also unto her husband with her; and he did eat.[2]

Why did Adam and Eve eat of the fruit? *Because the way seemed right.* It appeared harmless. As a result, they stood in their own way of living forever in the Garden of Eden. Can you imagine not having to engage in hard labor and enjoying everything nature has to offer without having to pay for it? Free water, free fruits and free vegetables - you can have a lion and an alligator as pets. How often do we stand in our own way of receiving God's best for our lives due to taking things lightly or making decisions because the way *seemed* right?

When things happen to us, often times we point the finger at others. However, the truth very well may be that we simply stood in our *own* way of being in God's direct will due to a bad decision, an act of faithlessness, or not taking the time to gather the facts before taking action.

There is a way that seemeth right but the end thereof is *not* death – but the *ways of death* for which death (spiritually, physically, or both) is the ultimate end. Well, what does that mean? The *ways of death* is another term for the "pathway to destruction". Simply stated, going in a way that *seems* right sets us on a course to destruction because ways that *seem* right by definition are unpromising and unreliable. A good barometer for one use in order to measure where they are going or how they may end up – is for them to look at what are doing both publicly and privately.

Conclusion:

For since the beginning of the world men have not heard, nor perceived by the ear, neither hath the eye seen, O God,

---

[2] *The Holy Bible: King James Version.* Ge 3:4–6.

beside thee, what he hath prepared for him that waiteth for him. [3]

Don't stand in your own way of being blessed by God.

Questions for discussion…

- How relevant are the scriptures for life today?

- The bible is clear regarding the penalties for living in disobedience. Why do you think some people still choose to live contrary to God's word?

- In the story of Adam and Eve, prior to eating the forbidden fruit, the serpent told Eve all the benefits of eating it but omitted the penalty. Whenever we are tempted, do you believe the same thing happens to us?

- What are some things we can do that will help us not to succumb to temptation?

Prayer Request…
Ask attendees if they have any prayer request…

Closing Prayer…
Below is a sample prayer that can be used or you can use your own incorporating the prayer request of the bible study attendees…

Dear God our Father, often we are making decisions without consulting you first. Often times we go off on our own and ignore what Your word says. On many fronts we

---

[3] *The Holy Bible: King James Version.* Is 64:4.

are guilty of going in a direction You don't approve of – and in the process have fallen out of Your direct will for our lives – and have found ourselves traveling a pathway to destruction. Forgive us for standing in our own way, no one else is to blame. Help us to be good stewards of all things – especially the choices we make. Not just the ones that impact us but also the ones that impact others – because even the penalty for this is potentially a path to destruction.

In Jesus name we pray, Amen.

LESSON 8
DEALING WITH DEFEAT

Agenda:
- Greeting and Opening Prayer
- Scripture
- Lesson
- Discussion
- Prayer Request
- Closing Prayer

Greeting and Prayer
Start session by welcoming attendees and saying an opening prayer. You may also ask one of the attendees if they would like to say the opening prayer.

Scripture ~ Psalms 46:1
[To the chief Musician for the sons of Korah, a song upon Alamoth.] God is our refuge and strength: a very present help in trouble.[1]

---

[1] *The Holy Bible: King James Version.* (2009). (Electronic Edition of the 1900 Authorized Version., Ps 46:1). Bellingham, WA: Logos Research Systems, Inc.

Into the lesson…

Most, if not all of us, have experienced defeat. There are times when experiencing defeat or losing occurs more frequently than being victorious. Some defeats we can brush off then move on with our lives but there are others we often times find it difficult to get over. Some defeats we do understand that with a little more effort or if we had made better decisions we could have come out on top. Yet, there are others that we yet experience although we've done our best. Regardless of how defeat may come our way and regardless of how major or minor it may be, for many, dealing with defeat can be difficult and rebounding from it can be a painful process.

Bearing this in mind, I am reminded of a young boy who attended a game of his favorite baseball team - the Detroit Tigers as they played the Oakland Athletics. While watching the game, he caught the grand slam homerun ball hit by Oakland. He was excited about the catch but the excitement soon turned into tears of sorrow when he looked at the scoreboard and saw that his team is losing as a result of the grand slam homerun souvenir ball he now held in his hands.[2]

Sometimes we can deal with our opponents hitting the ball over the fence as long as we are still ahead. But what do you do when you are the recipient of the grand slam homerun souvenir ball that puts your enemy ahead and causes them to win the game?

As we look at the text for this lesson, in it we find a reminder for when we also are dealing with defeat. This passage originated out of a time of great turmoil in Israel's

---

[2] Thomas Duffy. *Kid Catches Oakland Home Run Ball Then Pouts When He Realizes What It Means.*
http://bleacherreport.com/articles/2484521-kid-catches-oakland-home-run-ball-then-pouts-when-he-realizes-what-it-means (accessed June 7, 2015).

history but was later on captured and sent to the chief musician to be set to music for the sons of Korah, a song upon Alamoth[3]. The overall context of the singing of this passage was that "not just anybody could sing it." It was for the sons of Korah who were descendants of Aaron – which means they were Levites or preachers. The term, a song upon Alamoth means that it was to be sung in high pitch soprano (or high tenor) by a choir of virgins (young girls)… The uniqueness of this passage is that it provides encouragement and instills confidence in those who are experiencing challenges in life.

So, how do you deal with defeat? This passage provides for us four basic things we ought to remember that will help us to deal with defeat. First, we have the Creator to lean on. Second, God is our refuge. Third, God is our strength. Fourth and finally, God has proven Himself over and over.

When this Psalms starts off, the author says, God is our refuge and strength. The word God in the original language is the term Elohim which means – the God of the universe – the Creator. In other words, the one true God (is – present tense, while we are going through) is our refuge and strength. So, even while experiencing defeat – in this Psalms we are reminded that even while going through the storm, we have the God of the universe – the Creator of Heaven and earth to lean upon.

Often times when dealing with defeat or loss, we are faced with where to go and to whom to turn. In this same passage not only do we discover that we can turn to the one true God but also He is our refuge which means that He is our shelter… A refuge is a place you run to in order to get away from someone or something. The concept here is that we can go to God during the time of storm

---

[3] Charles H. Spurgeon. *The Treasury of David.* Spurgeon. Vol. 1. (Peabody: Hendrickson Publishers, 1996), 339.

and He will cover us from the elements. Not only is God the creator, and shelters us, but He is also strong – which means that He has the power to keep us or hold us. There are places or people you can run to for refuge but they are strong enough to protect us and therefore are not safe. But God is our refuge and strength – a very present help (which means that He has been proven to be faithful or has proved Himself over and over) in the time of trouble.

Closing:

Anybody experiencing some trouble, dealing with defeat? Anybody left holding the game winning grand slam homerun ball of their opponent? Just remember, the season is not over, there's another game to play. God is our refuge and our strength – a very present help in the time of trouble. This is a great way to deal with defeat!

Questions for discussion...

- Can you think of a few scriptures that will help deal with life's defeats? If so, what are they?

- To whom have you usually turned when life has gotten the best of you? Was the Lord the last person you consulted?

- The Lord has a proven record of redeeming us. Why, in so many instances, do people still fail to go to Him first when facing defeat?

- If people would turn to the Lord first, how much of a difference do you believe it would make regarding their outlook and how they respond to their situations? Why?

Prayer request…

Ask attendees if they have any prayer request…

Closing Prayer…

Below is a sample prayer that can be used or you can use your own incorporating the prayer request of the bible study attendees…

Dear God our Father, often we are challenged with overcoming defeat. Rather than turning to You, sometimes we try to fix the situation ourselves. Help us to remember that You are our refuge and strength and that You have a proven track record for rescuing us. Forgive us for the times we have failed to turn our situations over to You. Give a fresh anointing and a new outlook on our defeats that we may realize that although the game may have been lost, the series is not over. And in this, we can rejoice because the victory has been won in Your Son, Christ Jesus.

It is in His precious, mighty, and strong name we pray, Amen.

Rev. Dr. E. J. Fleming, Jr.

BIBLIOGRAPHY

Ben. *Faith vs. Trust,*
http://christianity.yoexpert.com/christianity-
general/what-is-the-difference-between-faith-and-
trust-20479.html (accessed May 13, 2015).

Duffy, Thomas. *Kid Catches Oakland Home Run Ball Then
Pouts When He Realizes What It Means,*
http://bleacherreport.com/articles/2484521-kid-
catches-oakland-home-run-ball-then-pouts-when-he-
realizes-what-it-means (accessed June 7, 2015).

Logos. *The Holy Bible: King James Version.* Electronic Edition
of the 1900 Authorized Version. Bellingham: Logos
Research Systems, Inc., 2009.

Spurgeon, Charles H. *The Treasury of David, Vol 1.* Peabody:
Hendrickson Publishers, 1996.

The Holy Bible: English Standard Version. Wheaton: Standard
Bible Society, 2001.

www.ingramcontent.com/pod-product-compliance
Lightning Source LLC
Chambersburg PA
CBHW061755040426
42447CB00011B/2306